The "Checklist"
By Anthony Uyl MTS

Devoted Publishing
Ingersoll, Ontario, Canada, 2023

The "Checklist"
By Anthony Uyl _{MTS}

Contact Us Online:

Email: office@devotedpub.com

For more information on Biblical Demonology and issues with the occult in modern evangelicalism, check out the authour' Substack Blog *Reformed Demonology*: https://reformeddemonology.substack.com

TABLE OF CONTENTS

THE "CHECKLIST"

In reality, there is only one thing you need to ask to see if songs from churches such as, not limited to but including: Hillsong, Bethel, Elevation, IHOP (and other Prosperity, Word-of-Faith and New Apostolic Reformation churches), and artists such as, not limited to but including, Chris Tomlin (and all other Prosperity, Word-of-Faith, and New Apostolic Reformation associated artists). That one question is this:

"Are they gospel believing repentant Christians?"

For any of the churches within the classification given above, the answer is a simple "no". The reason being that all those churches affirm that the Prosperity Gospel is the true gospel.[1] That gospel denies the atonement that is shown in the Bible and promotes a false Jesus. Therefore, by definition, these churches are classed as heretical. Chris Tomlin has likewise affirmed Word-of-Faith doctrine in interview articles many times.

Second, since not all these churches have the same Christology, many do still claim that Jesus did not use, or even have, his fully divine power while on earth. These churches claim that Jesus was just a man, and as a man, we can do the same things Jesus did.[2] This is known as the "kenotic heresy" and is heresy because if Jesus was

---

1. Brian Houston, *For This I Was Born* (Nashville, Tennessee: Thomas Nelson), pp. 129–130, Kindle Edition.

2. Kimberly Daniels, *Clean House, Strong House: A Practical Guide to Understanding Spiritual Warfare, Demonic Strongholds, and Deliverance* (Lake Mary, Florida: Charisma House, 2014), Logos Edition. And: Bill Johnson and Mike Seth, *When Heaven Invades Earth for Teens: Your Guide to God's Supernatural Power* (Shippensburg, Penn-sylvania: Destiny Image, 2014), Logos Edition.

not fully God in power while on earth, then he could not fulfill the requirements of the Christ given in the Old Testament.

Third, almost all of these churches and artists affirm the "little gods heresy". Despite the arguments given, the little gods teaching is a heresy because these churches/artists use it to claim their own divinity in that God must do what they "declare".

Fourth, these churches claim that they have no sin. These teachers say we can commit sin, but we "have" no sin in us.[3] This is a defilement of 1 John 1 and shows that they are in fact calling Jesus a "liar" as 1 John 1 says.

Lastly, any churches or persons that affirm same-sex relationships as unsinful, or abortion as unsinful are also not Christians in any way. These things are considered abominations in scripture and abortion is a Christological heresy because it would mean that Jesus was not human while in Mary's womb. Again, denying either Jesus as fully God in power and might, and the humanity of Jesus is a salvation denying heresy. All heresy is salvation denying.

As a side note: the argument that God can use sinful people is true. However, sinful people that are not in covenant with God, and not repentant for their sin are not by the biblical definition a believer in Christ. If someone is confronted about their sin and all the steps from Matthew 18:15–17 do not get that person to repent, then the last line of verse 17 applies that "let him be unto thee as an heathen man and a publican" (Matthew 18:17 KJV 1900). Basically, an unrepentant Christian, is not a Christian. This person may be "regenerate" to a point, but until they fully repent of gross biblical error, they are not to be considered part of the Christian (or covenant)

---

3. Kris Vallotton and Bill Johnson, *The Supernatural Ways of Royalty: Discovering Your Rights and Privileges of Being a Son or Daughter of God* (Shippensburg, Pennsylvania: Destiny Image, 2006), Logos Edition.

community.

Since, these churches and artists cannot be placed in a "Christian" covenant status, the following texts from Titus 1 applies:

> This witness is true. Wherefore rebuke them sharply, that they may be sound in the faith; Not giving heed to Jewish fables, and commandments of men, that turn from the truth. Unto the pure all things are pure: but unto them that are defiled and unbelieving is nothing pure; but even their mind and conscience is defiled. They profess that they know God; but in works they deny him, being abominable, and disobedient, and unto every good work reprobate (Titus 1:13–16 KJV 1900).

So, let me break this down more simply: if a person is a true biblically defined believer, even if they have committed sin, their work is sill considered pure. However, if someone is not a biblically defined believer, as was conditioned above, everything that person, or church, produces is "reprobate", bad, and condemned.

Paul, being an ex-Pharisee, knew very well, what a "pure" offering would consist of in Jewish law. Paul, as an apostle, carries over those commands to our acts of worship, or "reasonable service".

> I beseech you therefore, brethren, by the mercies of God, that ye present your bodies a living sacrifice, holy, acceptable unto God, which is your reasonable service. And be not conformed to this world: but be ye transformed by the renewing of your mind, that ye may prove what is that good, and acceptable, and perfect, will of God (Romans 12:1–2 KJV 1900).

So, what you offer as a "sacrifice", or as "worship", must be acceptable to God. Since Titus 1 clearly shows that what unbelievers produce is "reprobate", their work/songs cannot be classed as "acceptable to God", even if the "words are okay".

Note what else Paul has to say about this false righteousness, or "the words are okay" in 2 Corinthians 11, and then Jesus himself in Matthew 7:

> For such are false apostles, deceitful workers, transforming themselves into the apostles of Christ. And no marvel; for Satan himself is transformed into an angel of light. Therefore it is no great thing if his ministers also be transformed as the ministers of righteousness; whose end shall be according to their works (2 Corinthians 11:13–15 KJV 1900).

> Beware of false prophets, which come to you in sheep's clothing, but inwardly they are ravening wolves. Ye shall know them by their fruits. Do men gather grapes of thorns, or figs of thistles? Even so every good tree bringeth forth good fruit; but a corrupt tree bringeth forth evil fruit. A good tree cannot bring forth evil fruit, neither can a corrupt tree bring forth good fruit. Every tree that bringeth not forth good fruit is hewn down, and cast into the fire. Wherefore by their fruits ye shall know them (Matthew 7:15–20 KJV 1900).

This is interesting. These churches and artists are intentionally making themselves "appear" righteous so that they can get their "reprobate" work into our churches. Paul says it directly in 2 Corinthians 11. Also, Jesus warns us of this same thing by saying that these ravening wolves will "intentionally" wear sheep's clothing (or write "good words") to get their influence and work into the local "biblical" congregation.

Since our worship is considered an "offering" according to Romans 12:1–2, there is precedent to look back into the Old Testament to see what Paul would have meant. The book of Leviticus starts out by telling us what an appropriate "offering" is.

> And the LORD called unto Moses, and spake unto

> him out of the tabernacle of the congregation, saying,
> Speak unto the children of Israel, and say unto them,
> If any man of you bring an offering unto the Lord, ye
> shall bring your offering of the cattle, even of the herd,
> and of the flock. If his offering be a burnt sacrifice
> of the herd, let him offer a male without blemish: he
> shall offer it of his own voluntary will at the door of
> the tabernacle of the congregation before the Lord
> (Leviticus 1:1–3 KJV 1900).

Within the Hebrew here, the indication is that the male without blemish[4] was to come from the worshipper's own flock. The worshipper was not to bring something from someone else's flock, and especially not from outside the covenant community (in our case, outside of biblically gospel preaching churches). There were provisions for the poor who would not have had their own flocks to instead bring a pigeon or turtledove to be offered in place of a sheep, goat or cow (depending on the sacrifice requirements). But these birds could not be "bought" from a Gentile passing through, they had to come from the Israelite community itself.

While we often hear about the "heart" or "intentions" of worship, we never hear about what "form" of worship is appropriate, for very apparent reasons. No one wants to answer for the fact that songs from outside the community, that are considered "reprobate" by Paul, are being used as "acceptable". Note what happened to Aaron's two sons Nadab and Abihu, when they offered an inappropriate offering to God:

> And Nadab and Abihu, the sons of Aaron, took either
> of them his censer, and put fire therein, and put incense
> thereon, and offered strange fire before the Lord,
> which he commanded them not. And there went out
> fire from the Lord, and devoured them, and they died

4. Francis Brown, Samuel Rolles Driver, and Charles Augustus Briggs, *Enhanced Brown-Driver-Briggs Hebrew and English Lexicon* (Oxford: Clarendon Press, 1977), p. 1071.

before the LORD. Then Moses said unto Aaron, This is it that the LORD spake, saying, I will be sanctified in them that come nigh me, and before all the people I will be glorified. And Aaron held his peace. And Moses called Mishael and Elzaphan, the sons of Uzziel the uncle of Aaron, and said unto them, Come near, carry your brethren from before the sanctuary out of the camp. So they went near, and carried them in their coats out of the camp; as Moses had said. And Moses said unto Aaron, and unto Eleazar and unto Ithamar, his sons, Uncover not your heads, neither rend your clothes; lest ye die, and lest wrath come upon all the people: but let your brethren, the whole house of Israel, bewail the burning which the LORD hath kindled. And ye shall not go out from the door of the tabernacle of the congregation, lest ye die: for the anointing oil of the LORD is upon you. And they did according to the word of Moses (Leviticus 10:1–7 KJV 1900).

Note the severity of the wrongful offering here. Nadab and Abihu are struck down from the altar in full view of the public. Also, Aaron and his surviving sons were not allowed to even touch, or mourn for the dead (as the law commanded they do) because what Nadab and Abihu had done was such an abomination before God. The remaining sons had to use their coats to carry their dead brothers out to not risk touching them.

There is also something else interesting going on with Nadab and Abihu here. While the fire these two men offered was "strange fire" that was forbidden before God, they were also making an offering that only the high priest, their father Aaron at the time could make. This "bad offering" was an attempt to usurp the high priest and the commands of God.

Who is the current high priest?

Seeing then that we have a great high priest, that is passed into the heavens, Jesus the Son of God, let us hold fast our profession. For we have not an high priest which cannot be touched with the feeling of our infirmities; but was in all points tempted like as we are, yet without sin. Let us therefore come boldly unto the throne of grace, that we may obtain mercy, and find grace to help in time of need (Hebrews 4:14–16 KJV 1900).

That is right. The current high priest is the second person of the Trinity, our Saviour, Jesus Christ. By offering "reprobate" sacrifices from outside the covenant community, not only are you disobeying the commands of scripture, but you are also attempting to usurp Jesus' role as high priest. That is very serious.

Note that, while in the text this is not chronological, the text of Leviticus 16 shows that the below commands happened immediately after Nadab and Abihu were judged by God.

And the LORD spake unto Moses after the death of the two sons of Aaron, when they offered before the LORD, and died; And the LORD said unto Moses, Speak unto Aaron thy brother, that he come not at all times into the holy place within the vail before the mercy seat, which is upon the ark; that he die not: for I will appear in the cloud upon the mercy seat. Thus shall Aaron come into the holy place: with a young bullock for a sin offering, and a ram for a burnt offering. He shall put on the holy linen coat, and he shall have the linen breeches upon his flesh, and shall be girded with a linen girdle, and with the linen mitre shall he be attired: these are holy garments; therefore shall he wash his flesh in water, and so put them on. And he shall take of the congregation of the children of Israel two kids of the goats for a sin offering, and one ram for a burnt offering. And Aaron shall offer his bullock of the sin offering, which is for himself, and make an atonement for himself, and for his house. And he shall take the two goats, and present

> them before the Lord at the door of the tabernacle of the congregation. And Aaron shall cast lots upon the two goats; one lot for the Lord, and the other lot for the scapegoat. And Aaron shall bring the goat upon which the Lord's lot fell, and offer him for a sin offering. But the goat, on which the lot fell to be the scapegoat, shall be presented alive before the Lord, to make an atonement with him, and to let him go for a scapegoat into the wilderness. And Aaron shall bring the bullock of the sin offering, which is for himself, and shall make an atonement for himself, and for his house, and shall kill the bullock of the sin offering which is for himself: And he shall take a censer full of burning coals of fire from off the altar before the Lord, and his hands full of sweet incense beaten small, and bring it within the vail: And he shall put the incense upon the fire before the Lord, that the cloud of the incense may cover the mercy seat that is upon the testimony, that he die not (Leviticus 16:1–13 KJV 1900).

This offering at the time was purposing two things: the first was the yearly observance of the Day of Atonement, but secondly, it was to purify the tabernacle and the entire Israelite community of the abomination committed by Nadab and Abihu. What Aaron's two dead sons had done was so horrid before God that the entire community needed to be cleansed, immediately. But Aaron, and future high priests, had to do and offer the right "offerings" or be struck down dead as well. Essentially, the defilement of God's commands, and the attempt to usurp the high priest (in our day Jesus), it falls into the same category of sin that the serpent tempted Adam and Eve into:

> And the serpent said unto the woman, Ye shall not surely die: For God doth know that in the day ye eat thereof, then your eyes shall be opened, and ye shall be as gods, knowing good and evil (Genesis 3:4–5 KJV 1900).

By not following the commands of the Bible, in both the Old and New Testaments, concerning our worship offerings, it is considered the same self-deifying act that got humanity condemned for all time, until Jesus made the atoning sacrifice of his own self. Realize how serious this is. By using the music from heretical churches and artists for "worship" that God considers "reprobate" you are in fact, declaring yourself to be higher than the entire Godhead and especially the high priest, Jesus.

But the condemnation for reprobate sacrifices is amplified in the new covenant. In the book of Malachi, which was the last book of the Old Testament written, Malachi looks forward to the new covenant but sternly warns that:

> But cursed be the deceiver, which hath in his flock a male, And voweth, and sacrificeth unto the Lord a corrupt thing: For I am a great King, saith the LORD of hosts, And my name is dreadful among the heathen (Malachi 1:14 KJV 1900).

Observing the text directly, what we have here is that a person is considered a deceiver who has offerings (or songs) that are perfectly fine in where they come from and are considered unblemished and perfect according to Old Testament and New Testament standards but offers what is "reprobate" instead. So, we as biblical Christians have a plethora of music available to us that has no controversy attached to it and is coming from churches and artists we can affirm are indeed "Christians", yet we decide to usurp the commands of God and Jesus our high priest, by offering what is "corrupt" instead.

Let me take a second to explain the issue with the word "cursed". In the Old Testament law, the word "curse" that is often used by these heretical churches to teach about "generational curses" is not speaking of something supernatural. Instead, the word is:

קָלַל (qālal) – despise, dishonour, made to feel worthless (Leviticus 24:14)[5]

The way that God carries out this curse is indicated in the three pieces of scripture below:

> Bring forth him that hath cursed without the camp; and let all that heard him lay their hands upon his head, and let all the congregation stone him. And thou shalt speak unto the children of Israel, saying, Whosoever curseth his God shall bear his sin. And he that blasphemeth the name of the LORD, he shall surely be put to death, and all the congregation shall certainly stone him: as well the stranger, as he that is born in the land, when he blasphemeth the name of the LORD, shall be put to death (Leviticus 24:14–16 KJV 1900).

> Behold, I set before you this day a blessing and a curse; A blessing, if ye obey the commandments of the LORD your God, which I command you this day: And a curse, if ye will not obey the commandments of the LORD your God, but turn aside out of the way which I command you this day, to go after other gods, which ye have not known (Deuteronomy 11:26–28 KJV 1900).

> But it shall come to pass, if thou wilt not hearken unto the voice of the LORD thy God, to observe to do all his commandments and his statutes which I command thee this day; that all these curses shall come upon thee, and overtake thee: Cursed shalt thou be in the city, and cursed shalt thou be in the field. Cursed shall be thy basket and thy store. Cursed shall be the fruit of thy body, and the fruit of thy land, the increase of thy kine, and the flocks of thy sheep. Cursed shalt thou be when thou comest in, and cursed shalt thou be when thou goest out. The LORD shall send upon thee cursing, vexation, and rebuke, in all that thou settest

---

5. Brown, *Hebrew*, p. 886.

thine hand unto for to do, until thou be destroyed, and until thou perish quickly; because of the wickedness of thy doings, whereby thou hast forsaken me. The LORD shall make the pestilence cleave unto thee, until he have consumed thee from off the land, whither thou goest to possess it. The LORD shall smite thee with a consumption, and with a fever, and with an inflammation, and with an extreme burning, and with the sword, and with blasting, and with mildew; and they shall pursue thee until thou perish. And thy heaven that is over thy head shall be brass, and the earth that is under thee shall be iron. The LORD shall make the rain of thy land powder and dust: from heaven shall it come down upon thee, until thou be destroyed. The LORD shall cause thee to be smitten before thine enemies: thou shalt go out one way against them, and flee seven ways before them: and shalt be removed into all the kingdoms of the earth (Deuteronomy 28:15–25 KJV 1900).

This means that the curse that God enacted on the pagan Israel was to humiliate them by sending them into exile. This specific curse was not some supernatural demonic and generational bondage that needed to be broken. It was a punishment given by God for idolatry or offering bad worship in our day.

However, Malachi uses a different word for curse in Malachi 1:14.

אָרַר (ārar) – a supernatural curse (judgment via the demonic) (Malachi 1:14)[6]

This changes things, now, anyone in the new covenant that offers something to God that is unacceptable/ reprobate instead of what is good, risks a serious supernatural/demonic curse/bondage. Those that have lived with true demonic judgment at the hands of God will tell you that they would rather have been allowed

---

6. Brown, *Hebrew*, p. 76.

to die than to have gone through that. It is not a pleasant experience for them.

Something else changes as well. The world for "blemish" or "corrupt thing" is made more severe as well. Instead of just an animal that was marked up and/or sick, these "corrupt things" under the new covenant have the word shākhat used which means two linked things. Since these two (the second being shakhat without the long "a" sound) words share the same consonantal root, they mean related and similar things to one another.[7]

שָׁחַת (shākhat) – more cursed/defiled[8]

שַׁחַת (shakhat) – something from the pit (Sheol)/underworld[9]

So, "corrupt", or "reprobate", sacrifices, under Paul's definition, under the new covenant are considered to be from the pits of Sheol/the underworld, or magical/necromantic in origin. Since Hillsong, Bethel and other such churches do teach an occultic form of biblical doctrine,[10] it should not be surprising that all of their ilk are considered to have written song "offerings" that are of one of the worst sins the law and the New Testament have to mention.

It does not really matter what the "heart" or "intention" is when using this music. See what happened to Uzzah in 2 Samuel.

---

7. Gary D. Pratico and Miles V. Van Pelt, *Basics of Biblical Hebrew Grammar, Third Edition* (Grand Rapids, Michigan: Zondervan, 2019), p. 115.

8. William Lee Holladay and Ludwig Köhler, *A Concise Hebrew and Aramaic Lexicon of the Old Testament* (Leiden: Brill, 2000), p. 366.

9. Holladay, *Hebrew*, p. 367.

10. Anthony Uyl, *The Emergence of the Neo-Satanist Church: The Reality of the Prosperity, Hillsong, Word-of-Faith, and New Apostolic Reformation Death Cult* (Ingersoll, Ontario, Canada: Devoted Publishing, 2023), pp. 47–61, 69–99.

Again, David gathered together all the chosen men of Israel, thirty thousand. And David arose, and went with all the people that were with him from Baale of Judah, to bring up from thence the ark of God, whose name is called by the name of the LORD of hosts that dwelleth between the cherubims. And they set the ark of God upon a new cart, and brought it out of the house of Abinadab that was in Gibeah: and Uzzah and Ahio, the sons of Abinadab, drave the new cart. And they brought it out of the house of Abinadab which was at Gibeah, accompanying the ark of God: and Ahio went before the ark. And David and all the house of Israel played before the LORD on all manner of instruments made of fir wood, even on harps, and on psalteries, and on timbrels, and on cornets, and on cymbals. And when they came to Nachon's threshingfloor, Uzzah put forth his hand to the ark of God, and took hold of it; for the oxen shook it. And the anger of the LORD was kindled against Uzzah; and God smote him there for his error; and there he died by the ark of God. And David was displeased, because the LORD had made a breach upon Uzzah: and he called the name of the place Perez-uzzah to this day. And David was afraid of the LORD that day, and said, How shall the ark of the LORD come to me? So David would not remove the ark of the LORD unto him into the city of David: but David carried it aside into the house of Obed-edom the Gittite. And the ark of the LORD continued in the house of Obed-edom the Gittite three months: and the LORD blessed Obed-edom, and all his household (2 Samuel 6:1–11 KJV 1900).

While many Christians have wondered why God struck Uzzah down for doing something out of the goodness of his heart, with the best intentions, Uzzah still violated the commands of the law concerning the ark of the covenant and was struck down for it. Good intentions do not always mean that our "worship" because the "words are okay" is not an abomination to God because we are offering these "reprobate" songs with a "good" heart.

Going back to the Matthew 7 verse above, you can see that a bad tree (heart) produces bad fruit, even if you may be doing it with the "right intention". Jesus has more to say in Mark 7 about this:

> And when he had called all the people unto him, he said unto them, Hearken unto me every one of you, and understand: There is nothing from without a man, that entering into him can defile him: but the things which come out of him, those are they that defile the man. If any man have ears to hear, let him hear. And when he was entered into the house from the people, his disciples asked him concerning the parable. And he saith unto them, Are ye so without understanding also? Do ye not perceive, that whatsoever thing from without entereth into the man, it cannot defile him; Because it entereth not into his heart, but into the belly, and goeth out into the draught, purging all meats? And he said, That which cometh out of the man, that defileth the man. For from within, out of the heart of men, proceed evil thoughts, adulteries, fornications, murders, Thefts, covetousness, wickedness, deceit, lasciviousness, an evil eye, blasphemy, pride, foolishness: All these evil things come from within, and defile the man (Mark 7:14–23 KJV 1900).

Realize what Jesus is saying: what is in your heart, comes out in your words and actions. So, if you are singing "reprobate" music because you have the best "intentions" and that it is okay because of "the words", Jesus is telling you that your heart contains "evil thoughts", "deceit", "wickedness", "blasphemy" and more. Again, the Bible has defined that what is not of the covenant community is "reprobate" and singing these songs shows that your heart is not good in any way. Listening to the music is not the problem, offering it as a "worship offering" is what shows that your heart is full of "wickedness", despite what your "intentions" are.

Revelation 22, the final words of Jesus spoken in our Bibles, tell us what will happen to those that "loveth and maketh a lie":

> Blessed are they that do his commandments, that they may have right to the tree of life, and may enter in through the gates into the city. For without are dogs, and sorcerers, and whoremongers, and murderers, and idolaters, and whosoever loveth and maketh a lie (Revelation 22:14–15 KJV 1900).

Realize the extreme nature of the condemnation here. When singing these "reprobate" worship songs, as Malachi shows, they are now in the new covenant considered to be as heinous as magic/necromancy which the above passage from Revelation shows, singing these songs, risks leaving you outside the kingdom. Also, when defending these songs because "the words are okay", despite the fact Paul in Titus 1 calls these songs "reprobate", it is evidence, by Jesus' statement in Mark 7 that you loveth a lie and that means deceit and wickedness are in your heart. All these things will leave you outside the kingdom. That is an extremely big risk to take for what essentially comes down to your own prideful self-gratification about the music you want to sing and not what God commands.

The next section from Matthew 7, for me, is the most terrifying of all of scripture:

> Not every one that saith unto me, Lord, Lord, shall enter into the kingdom of heaven; but he that doeth the will of my Father which is in heaven. Many will say to me in that day, Lord, Lord, have we not prophesied in thy name? and in thy name have cast out devils? and in thy name done many wonderful works? And then will I profess unto them, I never knew you: depart from me, ye that work iniquity. Therefore whosoever heareth these sayings of mine, and doeth them, I will liken him unto a wise man, which built his house

upon a rock: And the rain descended, and the floods came, and the winds blew, and beat upon that house; and it fell not: for it was founded upon a rock. And every one that heareth these sayings of mine, and doeth them not, shall be likened unto a foolish man, which built his house upon the sand: And the rain descended, and the floods came, and the winds blew, and beat upon that house; and it fell: and great was the fall of it (Matthew 7:21–27 KJV 1900).

This is terrifying. By singing these songs (which are "reprobate", Titus 1), which shows you love a lie and deception (Revelation 22), and that it shows your true heart condition (Mark 7), it does not matter what your intentions are according to Matthew 7:21–27. Those that "work iniquity" are asking Jesus himself, "did we not do all these things in your name and for you?" Yet, because of the iniquity/sin in their heart, shown by what they do and say, and sing, Jesus tells them, "I never knew you." That is an awfully big risk to take for the sake of singing what is "reprobate".

If you think that God will just "let it slide", then the testimony of history is lost on you. Even in the last one-hundred years alone we can name several individual churches that have closed their doors permanently because of their "reprobate" offerings (not just songs, but heretical teaching). Not only that, but we can also look back and see entire denominations that no longer exist for the exact same thing even in the last one-hundred years. God will act and judge those that are singing iniquity every Sunday. It is only a matter of time before God gets frustrated with his holy name being blasphemed by "well intentioned" people like Uzzah in our church's music teams and leadership.

Remember these final words of Christ:

He which testifieth these things saith, Surely I come quickly. Amen. Even so, come, Lord Jesus (Revelation

22:20 KJV 1900).

Will Jesus be coming to your church for judgment or blessing? Will you greet him with true praises or the reprobate songs of heretical churches?

Stop singing these songs.

With the latest article that has shown that these same churches have now "declared" that since they are the "chosen of God" that they need to physically attack the poor, with the goal of beating them into "wealth" so that these churches version of "heaven"[11] (really hell),[12] will come down to earth, whenever these songs are being used in Sunday morning worship, it is now literally blood-money being paid to these heretical churches for the sake of your "good intentions". How many people are going to have to be seriously hurt physically, as if enough people have not already been financially, relationally, emotionally, and spiritually hurt, before the blood money is too much to pay to continue to associate with these heretics?

For the full article, see here:

https://www.msn.com/en-ca/news/world/growing-strain-of-evangelicalism-preaches-hostility-towards-poor-americans-report/ar-AA1iHQRL?ocid=socialshare&pc=U531&cvid=fc4e3a08fffe4b23933fc679b87d2d66&ei=17

Now that money is involved in the usurping of Christ, more relevant passages start to emerge. First, we have:

> And I said unto them, If ye think good, give me my price; and if not, forbear. So they weighed for my price thirty pieces of silver. And the LORD said unto me, Cast it unto the potter: a goodly price that I was prised at of them. And I took the thirty pieces of silver, and cast them to the potter in the house of the LORD. Then I cut asunder mine other staff, even Bands, that

---

11. Johnson, *Heaven*, Logos Edition.
12. Uyl, *Emergence*, pp. 140–155.

> I might break the brotherhood between Judah and
> Israel (Zechariah 11:12–14 KJV 1900)

Also

> If the ox shall push a manservant or a maidservant;
> he shall give unto their master thirty shekels of silver,
> and the ox shall be stoned (Exodus 21:32 KJV 1900).

Ironically, the price of a man/maidservant (or a "slave") in the Old Testament Mosaic law was thirty pieces/shekels of silver. For the price of a slave, the unity between Israel (a pagan nation after their separation from Judah) and Judah, would be broken. Seeing that connection then the betrayal of Judas, a disciple of Jesus becomes more evident.

> Then one of the twelve, called Judas Iscariot, went
> unto the chief priests, And said unto them, What will
> ye give me, and I will deliver him unto you? And they
> covenanted with him for thirty pieces of silver. And
> from that time he sought opportunity to betray him
> (Matthew 26:14–16 KJV 1900).

After Judas's betrayal the guilt was too much, and he tried to return the silver. However, the men that hired Judas, as a slave, in their response to Judas returning the silver he was paid to betray Jesus has some fascinating similarities to evangelical churches and the way they use Prosperity music.

> Then Judas, which had betrayed him, when he saw
> that he was condemned, repented himself, and brought
> again the thirty pieces of silver to the chief priests and
> elders, Saying, I have sinned in that I have betrayed
> the innocent blood. And they said, What is that to
> us? see thou to that. And he cast down the pieces
> of silver in the temple, and departed, and went and
> hanged himself. And the chief priests took the silver
> pieces, and said, It is not lawful for to put them into

the treasury, because it is the price of blood. And they took counsel, and bought with them the potter's field, to bury strangers in. Wherefore that field was called, The field of blood, unto this day. Then was fulfilled that which was spoken by Jeremy the prophet, saying, And they took the thirty pieces of silver, the price of him that was valued, whom they of the children of Israel did value; And gave them for the potter's field, as the Lord appointed me (Matthew 27:3–10 KJV 1900).

I hope the connection here is clear. Evangelical churches are giving their money (silver) to Prosperity churches, for music that betrays (usurps) the real high priest's authority. In return, the Prosperity churches are now targeting the poor ("strangers", or non-Jews, whom the Prosperity movement would call the "unchosen" and "non-Christians") to "bury" them because they are not worthy of being among them because, according to the article linked above, the poor are not the "Chosen Ones".

Evangelical churches are selling out the Lord they claim to worship and praise, for less than the price of a "slave" or "servant".

Jesus' condemnation for this is extremely harsh.

Now when the even was come, he sat down with the twelve. And as they did eat, he said, Verily I say unto you, that one of you shall betray me. And they were exceeding sorrowful, and began every one of them to say unto him, Lord, is it I? And he answered and said, He that dippeth his hand with me in the dish, the same shall betray me. The Son of man goeth as it is written of him: but woe unto that man by whom the Son of man is betrayed! it had been good for that man if he had not been born. Then Judas, which betrayed him, answered and said, Master, is it I? He said unto him, Thou hast said (Matthew 26:20–25 KJV 1900).

Revelation 22 and Matthew 7 show that people that love

"lies" and that think they are doing what Christ wants even though the commands of scripture above clearly show that what they are doing with singing these songs because "the words are okay", will be left outside the kingdom and told by Christ "I never knew you". It would truly be best if these so-called "faithful" Christians had never been born. These "faithful" Christians because the "words are okay" are selling out their "lord" to evil people for money. These "faithful" Christians are not even the ones being paid to betray Jesus, they are paying a false church so that they can betray and usurp the very man and God they call "king".

I will leave this with one final piece of scripture.

> For this ye know, that no whoremonger, nor unclean person, nor covetous man, who is an idolater, hath any inheritance in the kingdom of Christ and of God. Let no man deceive you with vain words: for because of these things cometh the wrath of God upon the children of disobedience. Be not ye therefore partakers with them. For ye were sometimes darkness, but now are ye light in the Lord: walk as children of light: (For the fruit of the Spirit is in all goodness and righteousness and truth;) Proving what is acceptable unto the Lord. And have no fellowship with the unfruitful works of darkness, but rather reprove them. For it is a shame even to speak of those things which are done of them in secret. But all things that are reproved are made manifest by the light: for whatsoever doth make manifest is light (Ephesians 5:5–13 KJV 1900).

Do the right and biblical thing. Stop usurping Christ, stop usurping the Trinity. Stop proudly proclaiming the darkest of sin in your hearts every Sunday thinking it is "just fine".

God's word says it is in fact, not "just fine".

God wills it.
Deus Lo Vult.

BIBLIOGRAPHY

Brown, Francis, Samuel Rolles Driver, and Charles Augustus Briggs. *Enhanced Brown-Driver-Briggs Hebrew and English Lexicon.* Oxford: Clarendon Press, 1977.

Daniels, Kimberly. *Clean House, Strong House*: *A Practical Guide to Understanding Spiritual Warfare, Demonic Strongholds, and Deliverance.* Lake Mary, Florida: Charisma House, 2014. Logos Edition.

Holladay, William Lee, and Ludwig Köhler, *A Concise Hebrew and Aramaic Lexicon of the Old Testament.* Leiden: Brill, 2000.

Houston, Brian. *For This I Was Born.* Nashville, Tennessee: Thomas Nelson. Kindle Edition.

Johnson, Bill, and Mike Seth. *When Heaven Invades Earth for Teens*: *Your Guide to God's Su-pernatural Power.* Shippensburg, Pennsylvania: Destiny Image, 2014. Logos Edition.

Pratico, Gary D., and Miles V. Van Pelt. *Basics of Biblical Hebrew Grammar*, Third Edition. Grand Rapids, Michigan: Zondervan, 2019.

Reed, Brad. "Growing strain of evangelicalism preaches 'hostility' towards poor Americans: Report." *MSN News*. Accessed October 30, 2023. https://www.msn.com/en-ca/news/world/growing-strain-of-evangelicalism-preaches-hostility-towards-poor-americans-report/ar-AA1iHQRL?ocid=socialshare&pc=U531&cvid=fc4e3a08fffe4b23933fc679b87d2d66&ei=17.

Uyl, Anthony. *The Emergence of the Neo-Satanist Church: The Reality of the Prosperity, Hillsong, Word-of-Faith, and New Apostolic Reformation Death Cult.* Ingersoll, Ontario, Canada: Devoted Publishing, 2023.

Vallotton, Kris, and Bill Johnson. *The Supernatural Ways of Royalty: Discovering Your Rights and Privileges of Being a Son or Daughter of God.* Shippensburg, Pennsylvania: Destiny Image, 2006. Logos Edition.